stuck lead.

the places we get stuck &
the God who sets us free

jennie allen

HarperChristian
Resources

Stuck Leader's Guide
© 2014 by Jennie Allen

Requests for information should be addressed to:
HarperChristian Resources, 3900 Sparks Dr. SE, Grand Rapids, Michigan 49546

ISBN 978-0-529-10999-6 (softcover)
ISBN 978-0-5291-1799-1 (ebook)

HarperChristian Resources titles may be purchased in bulk for church, business, fundraising, or ministry use. For information, please e-mail ResourceSpecialist@ChurchSource.com.

First Printing February 2014 / Printed in the United States of America

contents

introduction

Leaders,

I am excited to partner with you in your efforts to pour into the lives of women! I pray that these few short pages will help to equip and prepare you to lead this study. Many of you may have led plenty of groups in the past, or perhaps this is the first you've led. Whichever the case, this is a spiritual calling and you are entering spiritual places with these women—and spiritual callings and places need spiritual power.

My husband, Zac, always says, "Changed lives, change lives." If you are not first aware of your own need for life change, the women around you won't see their need. If you allow God into the inner struggles of your heart, the women following you will be much more likely to let Him into theirs. These women do not need to see bright and shiny, perfectly poised people; they need to see people who are a mess and daily dependent on God for their hope and strength.

Over and over again in Scripture we see God drawing near to the brokenhearted. On earth, Jesus moved toward sinners, saying things like, "Those who are well have no need of a physician, but those who are sick. I came not to call the righteous, but sinners" (Mark 2:17). So if you feel inadequate, as though you have no business leading a group of women, be encouraged; you are just the kind of person God wants to use!

I visited a halfway house once. All of the men were just out of prison. And with tears they confessed truly owning their weaknesses and mistakes. Their hearts were bleeding for the damage they had brought to those they love and gushing at how God had forgiven them.

I wanted to be like them—these men recovering from the consequences of sin. I wanted to need God like they did, feel broken like they were, and be transparent like they were. It was as if they were already exposed . . . already caught. "Screwed up" was written on their foreheads; they saw no need to act like it wasn't. And something about that brought freedom.

It's troubling to feel broken. It is troubling to need God. But we begin as leaders with humility as our posture. We begin with repentance because all of us have sin, even if it is invisible. Pray and confess the sin that you see within yourself, and ask God for His forgiveness. It will be easy for women to follow a humble leader who also needs God.

For this people's heart has become calloused; they hardly hear with their ears, and they have closed their eyes. Otherwise they might see with their eyes, hear with their ears, understand with their hearts and turn, and I would heal them.

matthew 13:15 NIV

God wants to turn and heal us, but we must live sensitive to His Spirit and in awareness of our need for Him.

what's in the box

Each *Stuck* kit includes:

see. A DVD with eight sessions

study. A copy of the study guide (each member of your group will need her own study guide). Additional study guides can be purchased separately (ISBN: 978-1-4185-4874-2).

lead. A copy of the leader's guide

ask. A set of conversation cards

If you have a large group of women and need to break down into smaller groups during your study times, you may want to purchase additional kits so each group can have access to a leader's guide and a set of conversation cards.

We will discuss how to use each element of this kit on pages 10–11.

the vision

1. That we would see the broken spots in our souls as the very places God most wants to meet us. He longs for humanity to see our need for Him.

For my power is made perfect in weakness.

2 corinthians 12:9 NIV

2. That we would obey God. God longs to free us, but we have to obey Him. And He makes no small request of us. It is found in one word: *die*. He calls us to die. Die to our plans for our lives, our expectations, our pride, our rights. And in dying we find life.

   To know God and to be full to the brim with Him . . . may that become our biggest goal.

For we know that our old self was crucified with [Christ] so that the body of sin might be done away with, that we should no longer be slaves to sin—because anyone who has died has been freed from sin.

romans 6:6–7 NIV

3. That women would be pointed to God, a God worth dying for. The rest of this leader's guide is aimed at equipping you to point the women of your group to God in ways that will change their lives.

preparing yourself to lead a group

1. **Pray:** Pray like the world is ending, pray like this is the last chance for people to know Him, pray like our lives and futures depend on it, pray like the future of souls in heaven is at stake . . . Pray like you need God.

   Pray for your women:
   :: That God would show them the things holding them back and keeping them from freedom.
   :: That they would feel safe to open up and process.
   :: That they would want more of God and that God would meet them.
   :: That the conversation would be focused on God.
   :: That we would be humble displays of God's grace to these women.
   :: That God would come and fall on your time together.
   :: That many would come to a saving faith as they see God for who He is.

2. **Lean on God:** Allow the Holy Spirit to lead every moment together. We have provided you with tools that we will discuss in the next section; however, they are only tools to use as the Spirit leads you and your time together. God will have unique agendas for each of your groups as you depend on Him. Lean into your own weakness and into His strength and direction.

When Jesus left His disciples to go back to His Father in heaven, He said, "Don't go anywhere until you have the helper I will send you." We need to obey that same command. We don't begin until it is with the power of the Holy Spirit within us (see Acts 1:4–5). He is real and available and waiting to flood our lives and the lives around us as we serve and speak. But we have to wait for Him to speak, ask if we should speak and what we should speak, and ask what to do in different situations. God wants us to need Him and to depend on His Spirit. If this is not how you live on a daily basis, begin today.

3. **Be transparent:** If you choose not to be vulnerable, no one else will be. If you desire women to feel safe with you and your group, be vulnerable. This is not an optional assignment. This is your calling as you lead these women.

4. **Listen but also lead:** Listen as women share struggles. Some women are taking a tremendous risk in being vulnerable with you. Protect them by not interrupting and by instead empathizing. Do not feel the need to speak after each person shares. After most women have shared their answers to a question, turn it back to the scripture from the study guide, and help them process the truth and hope in their struggles. Avoid lecturing, but do bring the women back to truth.

5. **Model trust:** Show them how you are applying these difficult lessons. Ask God to convict you and lead out with how you are processing change in your own life.

the study

This study is uniquely designed to work in any venue or location. I envision women leading this in their homes, on campuses, even in their workplaces. Church buildings are the traditional format for group Bible studies, and *Stuck* will be effective inside the church walls, but the bigger dream is that women would find this study useful in reaching their friends, neighbors, and coworkers.

Whether you find yourself with 150 women in a church auditorium or with a few neighbors in your living room, this study is designed for small groups of women to process truth within their souls. Because of the depth of the questions and topics, it is essential that your group be small enough to share. A maximum of eight women in each group is ideal, preferably fewer. If you are in a larger group, divide into smaller groups with volunteer facilitators. With the help of the leader's guide and the Ask conversation cards, those smaller groups should still prove successful with a little support.

Session Tools and How to Use Them

See. These short, engaging videos are meant to set the tone for your time together, to draw women deeper into the Scripture, and to set the stage for transparent sharing. Hopefully, each person has already deeply studied the scriptures for themselves before coming to the group, and the video will provide enough to jump-start a powerful time of reflection and processing how to apply all they have learned in personal study that week. The videos are all under ten minutes.

Study. In the first meeting, distribute your group's study guides (or if women are purchasing on their own, remind them to bring their study guides to the first meeting). The lessons in the study guide (except for Lesson One) are meant to be completed during the week before coming to the group meeting. Each week begins with a short intro before moving into the portion marked "Study." The Study portion is followed by four application projects, then closing thoughts from me. The Study portion and projects can be completed in one sitting or broken up into smaller parts throughout the week, depending on each individual woman's needs.

These lessons may feel different from studies you have done in the past. They are very interactive. The goal of the curriculum is to lead women to dig deeply into Scripture and uncover how it applies to their lives, to deeply engage the mind and the heart. Projects, stories, and Bible study all play a role. The projects in the study guide will provide several options for applying Scripture. You and your group members may be drawing or journaling or interacting with the homeless in these projects. At the group meeting discuss your experience in working through the lesson.

Lead. This guide serves as a tool to prepare you in leading this study and to encourage you along the way. Refer back to it each week to be aware of the goals for each lesson. The leader's guide will help you effectively point your women to the overarching theme of each lesson and point them to the themes of the study.

Ask. These cards provide a unique way of starting deep, honest conversations about the places in which you are growing or feel stuck. Each week's cards are labeled with the appropriate lesson title. These should be pulled out after the DVD or teaching time.

1. Lay out the cards for the week, with the questions facing up.
2. Allow each woman to grab her favorite one.
3. Every week, go over the Ground Rules found in the front of the Ask deck of cards.
4. Begin by laying out the Scripture card for that week. Refer back to it as needed for help processing as you share.
5. Take turns having each woman ask the question on her card. Allow time for anyone who wants to share or respond to the question.
6. You may only get through a few of the questions. That is fine.

The goals of the questions are to allow women to reflect on what they have studied and heard and have a chance to share their own hearts. Again, do not be afraid to lead the discussion back to God if it feels as though things are getting off topic, but first allow everyone to concisely and clearly communicate their hearts. Several of the cards each week have scripture on them to help you do that. Pull one of those if you feel the group needs to hear what God says about the issues.

Session Format

This eight-week study is designed to go deep very quickly. Since women are busy and have full lives, the beauty of this study is it can be led in a living room over a one-hour lunch, or in a church Bible study spread out over two and a half hours. If you have the flexibility, extend the time of sharing in small groups. A frequent complaint is, "We wish we had more time to share." When the group is given deep questions and space to reflect and respond, you'll be surprised how beautiful and plentiful the conversations will be.

These tools are meant to have some flexibility. Here are some suggestions for how to structure your meeting to get the most out of your time together. However, you will be the best judge of what works for your group and the time you have together. Based on your group's needs, choose any combination of going through the questions mixed with reflections from group members' personal study.

Homework Discussion [20–35 minutes]:

After welcoming everyone and opening in prayer, you may choose to begin by having the women discuss their personal reflections as they have worked through the study guide and scripture that week. If you have more than eight members, break into small groups for this discussion time before reconvening for the video/teaching time.

Video and/or Teaching [10–40 minutes]:

Watch the DVD to provide a foundation for that week's lesson and to help transition to transparent sharing using the Ask conversation cards. If you are supplying teaching in addition to the videos, we recommend you begin with your teaching and then play the video.

Ask Conversation Cards [30–75 minutes]:

Especially if there are more than eight group members, divide into smaller groups and have women go through the Ask conversation cards. This will be a time of deep sharing and discussion that is important to learning how to apply all that has been learned that week.

leading your group: tips and things to watch out for

The study guide has the following information at the beginning. Review these guidelines carefully. During your first meeting, read through these expectations together as a group. Revisit these guidelines with the group in the coming weeks if necessary.

Get Honest

This is going to get messy, but it will be worth it. We will be dealing with hidden sin. God wants to do something with that. But until we recognize that we are stuck and in need of Him, we will miss what He has for us. If you consider yourself stuck, perhaps you would be willing to consider a way out, even if it is costly. Be honest with yourself and honest with God. He knows all of it already, anyway.

Engage with Your Small Group

Do not attempt to deal with such a large thing as sin without kindred warriors at your side, fighting with you and for you. Pray, speak truth in love, and hold each other's feet to the fire. Be vulnerable, and do not abandon those who are vulnerable with you. Prepare to go to war alongside these women. Keep your group a safe place to wrestle and discover and also a place filled with truth.

John described Christ as being "full of grace and truth" (John 1:14).
I pray this is how your small group will also be described.

And you shall know the truth, and the truth shall make you free.

john 8:32 NKJV

Commit to being consistent and present. Every time you gather
with your group, you will be building your view of God and His
plan for reconciliation in our lives. This study will create a circular
understanding of God and His plan, and missing a week will leave
a hole in that circle. Every time you are in your small group, you
will be processing God in your life. Consistency and presence show
respect to God and those around you in this process.

Please be quick to listen and slow to speak. Lean into the Holy Spirit
as you process together. Speak as He leads. This kind of vulnerable,
Spirit-led communication with your group will help lead to unstuck
lives.

Let every person be quick to hear, slow to speak.

james 1:19

Ground Rules for Discussion

:: *Be concise.* Share your answers to the questions while protecting others' time for sharing. Be thoughtful. Don't be afraid to share with the group, but try not to dominate the conversation.

:: *Keep group members' stories confidential.* Many things your group members share are things they are choosing to share with *you*, not with your husband or other friends. Protect each other by not allowing anything shared in the group to leave the group.

:: *Rely on Scripture for truth.* We are prone to use conventional, worldly wisdom as truth. While there is value in that, this is not the place. If you feel led to respond, please only respond with God's truth and Word, not "advice."

:: *No counseling.* Protect the group by not directing all attention on solving one person's problem. This is the place for confessing and discovery and applying truth together as a group. Your group leader will be able to direct you to more help outside the group time if you need it. Don't be afraid to ask for help.

What Stuck Is Not

We all are products of imperfect environments. Even with the best parents, spouses, and friends, we still have wounds from relationships. The hurt from these relationships takes work to process, and there are many great resources your group leader can suggest that take you deeper into the wounds from your past. I believe in the wisdom of Christian counseling, and there is a time and place for it. Christian counseling is a process I went through earlier in my life, and it truly brought so much freedom.

However, in *Stuck* the focus is intended to remain on God and His plan for us in eternity, and is not intended to be counseling. I believe growing in our perspective of who He is and what He has for us changes the way we view our past hurts and current struggles.

He heals the brokenhearted and binds up their wounds.

psalm 147:3 NKJV

Nothing is more powerful than God getting bigger in our lives. He has the power to heal with a word. My goal as you walk through *Stuck* is that God would get bigger for you and, as He does, you would see a new way to do life, led by His Spirit.

Guiding Conversation

You may come across some challenges when leading a group conversation. Normally these fall into two categories. In both situations people will need encouragement and grace from you as a leader. As with everything in this study, seek the Holy Spirit's guidance as you interact with your group members.

1. **Dominating the conversation:** If one woman seems to be dominating the conversation or going into detail that makes the rest of the group uncomfortable, gently interrupt her if necessary and thank her for sharing. Avoid embarrassing her in front of the group. Ask if there is anyone else who would like to share in response to the original question asked (not to necessarily respond to the woman who was just speaking). If the problem persists, talk with the woman outside of the group time. Affirm her for her vulnerability and willingness to share, and be prepared to refer her for more help if the need arises.

2. **Not sharing as much as the others:** If you notice there is a woman who seems to not be as talkative as the others in the group, you may try gently asking for her input directly at some point in the conversation. Some women are naturally shyer than others; don't try to force them into an extroverted role, but do let them know their input is valuable to the group. Remind them of the goals of the study and how being vulnerable with one another is one of the ways God shapes us spiritually. If a woman is just not interested in being in the study and is holding the rest of the group back, meet with her outside the group setting to discuss her further involvement.

Keep in mind that no two women are alike, but keep the best interests of the group in mind as you lead. For more information on two kinds of learners, see pages 20–21.

What Stuck Is Not: When to Refer

Some of the women in your care may be suffering past the point you feel able to help. This study may bring the pain of circumstances or behaviors to the surface. To leave women in this state would be more damaging than helpful. Don't try to take on problems you do not feel equipped to handle. If you sense that a woman may need more help, follow up and refer her to someone.

:: Check with your church or pastor for names of trusted Christian counselors. Some major indicators of this need would be: depression, anxiety, suicide, abuse, broken marriage. These are the obvious ones, but honestly, some women who are stuck in hurt from their past, minor depression, or fear could also benefit from counseling. I believe counseling is beneficial for many. So keep a stash of names for anyone you may feel needs to process further with a professional.

:: Look for the nearest Celebrate Recovery group, and offer to attend the first meeting with her (www.celebraterecovery.com).

:: Suggest further resources, and help to make a plan for her future growth and well-being.

:: Communicate with the leadership at your church about how to proceed with care.

:: Do not abandon these hurting women in a vulnerable place. This may be the first time they have opened up about painful hurts or patterns. Own their care, and see it through. If they have landed in your group, God has assigned them to you for this season, until they are trusted to the care of someone else. Even then, continue to check in on them.

types of learners

Hopefully, you will be blessed to be leading this study with a group diverse in age, experience, and style. While the benefits of coming together as a diverse group to discuss God outweigh the challenges by a mile, there are often distinctions in learning styles. Just be aware and consider some of the differences in two types of learning styles that may be represented. (These are obviously generalizations, and each woman as an individual will express her own unique communication style, but in general these are common characteristics.)

Experiential Learners

There are women who are more transparent, don't like anything cheesy, want to go deep quickly, and are passionate. Make a safe environment for them by being transparent yourself and engaging their hearts. These women may not care as much about head knowledge and may care more deeply how knowledge about God applies to their lives. They want to avoid being put in a box. Keep the focus on applying truth to their lives and they will stay engaged. Don't preach to them; be real, and show them through your experiences how to truly follow after God.

Pragmatic Learners

These women are more accustomed to a traditional, inductive, or precept approach to Bible study. They have a high value for truth and authority but may not place as high a value on the emotional aspects of confessing sin and being vulnerable. To them it may feel unnecessary or dramatic. Keep the focus on the truth of Scripture. These women keep truth in the forefront of their lives and play a valuable role in discipleship.

***

Because this study is different from traditional studies, some women may need more time to get used to the approach of this study. The goal is still to make God big in our lives, to know and love Him more, and to deal with sin by instructing with Scripture. These are the goals for all believers; we all just approach them in unique ways to reach unique types of people. I actually wrote this study praying it could reach both types of learners. I am one who lives with a foot in both worlds, trying to apply the deep truths I gained in seminary in an experiential way. I pray that this study would deeply engage the heart and the mind, and that we would be people who worship God in spirit and in truth, not just learning about sin but going to war with it together.

Common struggles, like fear, stress, anger, shame, and insecurity are not respecters of age, religion, or income level. These struggles are human, and I have seen *Stuck* transcend the typical boundaries of Christian and seeker, young and old, single and married, needy and comfortable, bringing these women together and to God in a unique and powerful way.

In the following pages and notes for each *Stuck* lesson, I hope I have given you enough guidance that you do not feel lost, but enough freedom to depend on the Holy Spirit. These are only suggestions, but hopefully these notes will help surface themes and goals to guide you through your discussion of group members' homework and through the discussion of the Ask conversation cards. The video, homework, and cards should provide more than enough material for great discussions, but stay on track, and be sure people are walking away with hope and truth.

getting started :: stuck

During this first meeting you will be getting to know each other, handing out the study guides, walking through the Instructions and Expectations (found on page 8 of the study guide), walking through the Getting Started lesson (found on page 13 of the study guide), and watching the first video.

Here are some general goals for your time together this week:

:: Make the women feel safe.

:: Get to know each other and the things you each struggle with.

:: Set expectations for the study.

:: Instruct group members on how to use the study guide and Ask conversation cards.

:: Create a need for this study in their lives by helping them see that we all struggle with inner, invisible things.

:: Stress that God longs for our freedom, and that freedom can be a reality in our lives.

LEADER: This first session's suggested format is different from the others' since it is your first meeting and there is no homework to review.

Video and/or Teaching

For this first meeting, it is best to begin by watching video session "Stuck."

Discussion Time

1. Together take some time to read the Introduction, Instructions and Expectations, and the Getting Started lesson in the study guide, either aloud or to yourselves, and discuss.

2. When you reach page 18 in the Getting Started lesson of the study guide, have participants choose the three places they feel most "stuck." Suggestions are included on the page in the study guide. Give everyone time to think about this and write down in their guides their three stuck places.

3. If you are in a large group, break into small groups and give each person the chance to open up about the three places she feels stuck. Leaders, share first, and be transparent.

4. After all the women have shared, you may transition to the Ask conversation cards to continue your discussion. The cards for this week are labeled "Stuck" on the front. Distribute this week's Ask cards, and guide the women to ask and answer the questions on the cards. Review the Ask card instructions together. Remember to begin with the Scripture card and end by stressing the scriptural truth group members can apply to their lives as a result of what they discussed in your group time. Close this discussion by praying for the things shared and praising God for His position in our lives and in eternity.

He who conceals his sins does not prosper, but whoever confesses and renounces them finds mercy.

proverbs 28:13 NIV

broken :: 1

This week we are studying the struggle between the Spirit and our flesh that has been warring since before God spun planets. We define this universal problem as the Spirit of life and peace versus the law of sin and death (Romans 8). We must begin here with the problem.

Here are some general goals for your time together this week:
:: Identify and define the war we all feel and see around us.
:: Help the women see their need for God, because of their sin.
:: Help the women come out of hiding behind pride or shame and confess the places of sin or hurt in their souls.
:: See God's plan and hope for sin and weakness in our lives.
:: Prepare to begin this journey humbly united in need of God.

Homework Discussion

Suggestions on places to focus as you go over the homework with your group:
:: Ask the group to share specifically about the war they studied in Romans 8.
:: Ask what they think God's goal is in allowing our weaknesses and neediness.
:: Discuss their response to Project 4.
:: Ask what else they learned as they studied and interacted with the lesson and Scripture this week.

Video and/or Teaching

Watch video session "Broken."

Ask Conversation Cards

If you are in a large group, break into small groups for discussion time using the Ask conversation cards. Distribute this week's Ask cards, and guide the women to ask and answer the questions on the cards. Remember to begin with the Scripture card and end by stressing the scriptural truth group members can apply to their lives as a result of what they discussed in your group time. Close this discussion by praying for the things shared and praising God for His position in our lives and in eternity.

"My grace is sufficient for you, for my power is made perfect in weakness." Therefore I will boast all the more gladly about my weaknesses, so that Christ's power may rest on me. That is why, for Christ's sake, I delight in weaknesses, in insults, in hardships, in persecutions, in difficulties. For when I am weak, then I am strong.

2 corinthians 12:9–10 NIV

mad :: 2

Anger is my reaction when my rights are being taken from me. We all live with basic assumptions about these rights. But Jesus calls us to a surrender that is so resolute, so final, that to lift our head in protest about our rights would seem insane. He laid down His rights in heaven and laid down His very life, being misunderstood by the world to the point of being brutally killed. And somehow, even though it feels like death, in laying down my rights, I find freedom.

LEADER: Take careful note to not imply that we are to endure abuse. You may have group members who have been physically, sexually, or otherwise abused in their pasts, or are being abused now. At the beginning of your time with the group, stress that God does not expect us to endure abuse, and offer to stay after the meeting to talk with anyone who needs help.

Here are some general goals for your time together this week:

:: Focus on the truth that the hidden rights we claim are often the source of anger and resentment when we feel threatened.
:: Point to the fact that Scripture calls us to lay down our rights over and over again.
:: Help the women see that in laying down our rights, we respond in a way that demonstrates God to our world.
:: Emphasize that in laying down our rights we find freedom from bitterness and resentment.
:: Remember that God is worth the abandonment of our rights.

Homework Discussion

Suggestions on places to focus as you go over the homework with your group:

:: How did the verses in James impact your view of anger?

:: What are some of the rights that you feel entitled to?

:: Look at the passage in Luke on page 43 in the study guide. How does this impact your view of our rights?

:: How did you feel in your home as a child in the presence of anger? Discuss Project 3.

Video and/or Teaching

Watch video session "Mad."

Ask Conversation Cards

If you are in a large group, break into small groups for discussion time using the Ask conversation cards. Distribute this week's Ask cards, and guide the women to ask and answer the questions on the cards. Remember to begin with the Scripture card and end by stressing the scriptural truth group members can apply to their lives as a result of what they discussed in your group time. Close this discussion by praying for the things shared and praising God for His position in our lives and in eternity.

If anyone would come after me, let him deny himself and take up his cross and follow me. For whoever would save his life will lose it, but whoever loses his life for my sake will find it. For what will it profit a man if he gains the whole world and forfeits his soul? Or what shall a man give in return for his soul?

matthew 16:24–26

---

discontent :: 3

Discontentment is plaguing the souls of women. Big things and small things—we want something more, something different. And our souls are sick about it. We are chasing wind. All the while, there is a giant story in the background that we can barely make out because we are so distracted. We are missing the point above it all . . . we are missing God, who wants to fill our discontented souls.

Here are some general goals for your time together this week:
:: Define the areas in which women are struggling with discontentment. These could be materialism, body image, and so on.
:: Come to an understanding that discontentment is sin and it is making us distracted and numb to God's bigger purposes. We are chasing the wind.
:: Help the women see that freedom from discontentment is found in delayed gratification—hoping for heaven.

We all long to be known and loved, and this desire often drives us to search in the wrong places. God created us with the desire to be known and loved, and only He can truly fill that desire.

Homework Discussion

Suggestions on places to focus as you go over the homework with your group:
:: What did you learn as you worked through Romans 12 and John 12?
:: What was your response to Katie's blog in Project 1?
:: Discuss your lists in Project 4.

Video and/or Teaching

Watch video session "Discontent."

Ask Conversation Cards

If you are in a large group, break into small groups for discussion time using the Ask conversation cards. Distribute this week's Ask cards, and guide the women to ask and answer the questions on the cards. Remember to begin with the Scripture card and end by stressing the scriptural truth group members can apply to their lives as a result of what they discussed in your group time. Close this discussion by praying for the things shared and praising God for His position in our lives and in eternity.

Whoever loves his life loses it, and whoever hates his life in this world will keep it for eternal life. If anyone serves me, he must follow me; and where I am, there will my servant be also. If anyone serves me, the Father will honor him.

john 12:25–26

scared :: 4

We worry about what we value. With no God, we value only what we see. We value today because it is all we have. But if that other kingdom is real and does last forever . . . something must change. We have to face what we fear. The bigger God gets, the less we live in fear.

Here are some general goals for your time together this week:

:: Develop an understanding that we worry about what we value and it often becomes an idol above God (e.g., people's approval, our children's behavior, our health, hobbies, money).

:: Help the women see that trust is the most obvious indicator that we truly believe in God. If we do not trust Him, we have to ask if we believe He loves us and that He is sovereign.

:: Challenge each other to die to your hopes for this life and receive whatever God has for you, even if it is difficult or costly.

:: Embrace the truth that we have to kill our idols and trust our God.

Homework Discussion

Suggestions on places to focus as you go over the homework with your group:

:: What did you learn about God and His love and care for you in Matthew 6?

:: What did you think of Isaiah 2? Do you see any idols in your life?

:: What amount of your thought life is tied up in worry or fear? Discuss Project 1.

:: Talk about what was in the blank at the bottom of Project 4.

Video and/or Teaching

Watch video session "Scared."

Ask Conversation Cards

If you are in a large group, break into small groups for discussion time using the Ask conversation cards. Distribute this week's Ask cards, and guide the women to ask and answer the questions on the cards. Remember to begin with the Scripture card and end by stressing the scriptural truth group members can apply to their lives as a result of what they discussed in your group time. Close this discussion by praying for the things shared and praising God for His position in our lives and in eternity.

The LORD is my shepherd. . . . Even though I walk through the valley of the shadow of death, I will fear no evil, for you are with me; your rod and your staff, they comfort me. . . . Surely goodness and mercy shall follow me all the days of my life, and I shall dwell in the house of the LORD forever.

psalm 23:1, 4, 6

overwhelmed :: 5

For many of us, busyness is our drug of choice. It makes us numb. We stay busy so that we don't have to think about anything too messy, too difficult. We don't want to feel our stuck places. Rather than depend on the Spirit to carry us along in our predestined journey, we allow the rope of our insignificant schedules to drag us under the boat—drowning us.

God charted our courses even before He created the foundations of the earth—our job is simply to live them out.

Here are some general goals for your time together this week:

:: Know that God prepared good deeds for us to carry out before time began (Ephesians 2:10).

:: Ask each other: Are you depending on the Holy Spirit to lead your minutes and days, or are you dependent on yourself?

:: See that God leading and empowering our actions is what separates the things that will last from the wasted things (1 Corinthians 3:11–15).

:: Know that God doesn't want us to do important, showy things; He wants us to simply obey Him (His Spirit inside of us and His word through Scripture) on a moment-by-moment basis.

:: The expectation throughout Scripture is that we would radically reorient our lives around the gospel and God's agenda upon our salvation. Ask each other: Have you rearranged your time and life?

NOTE: Before leaving this week, take a look at Project 4 in the next lesson (Sad) on page 121 of the study guide. Schedule that time together for this coming week.

Homework Discussion

Suggestions on places to focus as you go over the homework with your group:

:: What did you learn about God in Ephesians 2?

:: What are we to do according to 1 Peter 4? Why are we to do it?

:: Talk about Project 1 and the valuable things we are doing and the things that are wasted.

:: Dream together over Project 4.

Video and/or Teaching

Watch video session "Overwhelmed."

Ask Conversation Cards

If you are in a large group, break into small groups for discussion time using the Ask conversation cards. Distribute this week's Ask cards, and guide the women to ask and answer the questions on the cards. Remember to begin with the Scripture card and end by stressing the scriptural truth group members can apply to their lives as a result of what they discussed in your group time. Close this discussion by praying for the things shared and praising God for His position in our lives and in eternity.

For we are [God's] workmanship, created in Christ Jesus for good works, which God prepared beforehand, that we should walk in them.

ephesians 2:10

sad :: 6

We all know something is not right; and hear me, it is not right! Yet, we spend our thoughts, time, and money trying to make life right, comfortable, safe, happy. Maybe we are spending all of this energy on the wrong things. Romans 8:25 says, "If we hope for what we do not yet have, we wait for it patiently" (NIV).

Here are some general goals for your time together this week:

:: Understand that until Christ returns, sadness is a part of our lives and this planet.
:: Help the women to see that if our goal is happiness, we will never arrive at our goal and will never be able to grow up and obey God.
:: Remember that sadness points to our longing for heaven and for God. Draw near to Him in it.
:: Clearly define and talk about a believer's hope and how we can live hopeful today.

Homework Discussion

Suggestions on places to focus as you go over the homework with your group:

:: What did you learn in Romans 8?
:: Why is sadness okay? And what is our hope?
:: Talk about Projects 1 and 4.

Video and/or Teaching

Watch video session "Sad."

Ask Conversation Cards

If you are in a large group, break into small groups for discussion time using the Ask conversation cards. Distribute this week's Ask cards and guide the women to ask and answer the questions on the cards. Remember to begin with the Scripture card and end by stressing the scriptural truth group members can apply to their lives as a result of what they discussed in your group time. Close this discussion by praying for the things shared and praising God for His position in our lives and in eternity.

We look not to the things that are seen but to the things that are unseen. For the things that are seen are transient, but the things that are unseen are eternal.

2 corinthians 4:18

unstuck :: 7

Use this session as a chance to really hear from your women about how they have grown and what they need in order to move forward. Celebrate, pray, and challenge them as you conclude this journey together. Our stuck places are the very places that make us ache for God. These don't completely go away until heaven. But knowing more of God changes everything and begins to fill us.

Here are some general goals for your time together this week:

:: Understand that our freedom is found in dying to ourselves and trusting God.

:: Know that our hope is heaven, and anything less will disappoint.

:: Challenge each other to live out our mission, which is to obey God and live displaying the gospel.

:: Challenge each other to see that life is short; we should probably get after it, since we know how this all ends!

Homework Discussion

Suggestions on places to focus as you go over the homework with your group:

:: Look at John 15, and talk about the power of a relationship with God.

:: What changed in the new covenant in Jeremiah 31?

:: Look at the drawings in Project 1.

:: Spend time on Project 3. Have everyone share their answer to the question: What are you leaving behind and what are you moving toward? (This is one of the Ask cards for this week.)

Video and/or Teaching

Watch video session "Unstuck."

Ask Conversation Cards

If you are in a large group, break into small groups for discussion time using the Ask conversation cards. Distribute this week's Ask cards, and guide the women to ask and answer the questions on the cards. Remember to begin with the Scripture card and end by stressing the scriptural truth group members can apply to their lives as a result of what they discussed in your group time. Close this discussion by praying for the things shared and praising God for His position in our lives and in eternity.

For we know that our old self was crucified with [Christ] so that the body of sin might be done away with, that we should no longer be slaves to sin—because anyone who has died has been freed from sin.

romans 6:6–7 NIV

---

about the author

jennie allen

My passion is to inspire a new generation of women to encounter the invisible God. I love words, and I believe God uses them to heal souls and to reveal Himself to people. I graduated from Dallas Theological Seminary with a master's in biblical studies.

***

And while all that sounds pretty fancy . . . I am really just a mess of a girl, trying to figure out God, and why I seem to keep struggling with the same invisible issues I had in kindergarten. I am so blessed to serve alongside my husband, Zac, in ministry. We have four children.

Compel them to come in.

luke 14:23 ESV

thecompelproject.com